Pope John XXIII

Angelo Giuseppe Roncalli

Blessed Are the Peacemakers

1881–1963

Born in Sotto il Monte, Italy

Feast Day: October 11

Patron of Papal Delegates and the Second Vatican Council

"Blessed are the peacemakers, for they will be called children of God."
Matthew 5:9

Text by Barbara Yoffie
Illustrated by Chris Sharp

Liguori Publications
A Redemptorist Ministry

Dedication

To my family:
my parents Jim and Peg,
my husband Bill,
our son Sam and daughter-in-law Erin,
and our precious grandchildren
Ben, Lucas, and Andrew

To all the children I have had the privilege
of teaching throughout the years.

Imprimi Potest:
Kevin Zubel, CSsR, Provincial
Denver Province, the Redemptorists

Published by Liguori Publications, Liguori, Missouri 63057
To order, visit Liguori.org or call 800-325-9521.

ISBN (print): 978-0-7648-2868-3
ISBN (digital): 978-0-7648-7251-8

Liguori Publications, a nonprofit corporation, is an apostolate of the Redemptorists. To learn more about the Redemptorists, visit Redemptorists.com.

Printed in the United States of America
28 27 26 25 24 / 5 4 3 2 1
First Edition

Dear Parents and Teachers:

Saints and Me! is a six-set series of children's books about saints, including the: *Saints of North America* who served our homeland; *Saints of Christmas,* who teach us to love Jesus; *Saints for Families,* who modeled God's love within and for the domestic Church; *Saints for Communities,* who served Jesus through various roles and professions; and *Saints for Sacraments,* who showed great love for the sacraments.

The eight books in *Saints of the Beatitudes* (a word meaning "a list of blessings from God") introduce nine holy people who exemplify attributes Jesus articulated in his Sermon on the Mount. Faustina Kowalska's diary, *Divine Mercy in My Soul,* read by millions, helped spread God's message of mercy. Patrick, a missionary, brought Christianity to Ireland. Monica prayed her wayward son, Augustine, would return to the faith. He did and was canonized. Katharine Drexel abandoned her comfortable life to become a nun. Carlo Acutis shared his faith and love of the Eucharist through technology. Bernadette Soubirous experienced visions of the Blessed Virgin Mary. Pope John XXIII convoked the Second Vatican Council, hoping to revive the Church. Jude was an apostle of our Lord.

Which saint was captured by pirates and sold into slavery? Name the saints with back-to-back feast days (August 27–28). Who gave $20 million to build churches and schools? Who created a website about eucharistic miracles? Who did Jesus appear and speak to? Who said, "My job is to inform, not to convince"? Who wrote *Peace on Earth* in 1963? Who is the patron of impossible causes? Find out in the *Saints of the Beatitudes* set—part of the *Saints and Me!* series—and help children connect to the lives of the saints.

Introduce your children or students to *Saints and Me!* as they:

—**READ** about the lives of the saints and are inspired by their stories.

—**PRAY** to the saints for their intercession.

—**CELEBRATE** the saints and relate them to their lives.

Free activities for children to use with this book may be downloaded at Liguori.org.

The Beatitudes

Divine blessings Jesus names in his Sermon on the Mount

Matthew 5:3–12

Saints of the Beatitudes

Patrick

Blessed Are the Poor in Spirit (Verse 3)

Monica and Augustine

Blessed Are the Mournful (Verse 4)

Katharine Drexel

Blessed Are the Meek (Verse 5)

Carlo Acutis

Blessed Are the Righteous (Verse 6)

Faustina Kowalska

Blessed Are the Merciful (Verse 7)

Bernadette

Blessed Are the Pure of Heart (Verse 8)

Pope John XXIII

Blessed Are the Peacemakers (Verse 9)

Jude the Apostle

Blessed Are the Persecuted (Verses 10–12)

"When I grow up, I am going to be a priest," Angelo told his friends. And that is exactly what he did! Ordained in 1904, he served the people of God in many ways. Over the years, Fr. Roncalli was a bishop, archbishop, cardinal, and pope! As pope, he taught respect for all people and religions and worked for world peace.

The Roncalli family lived in a small stone building on a farm near Bergamo, Italy. Angelo was the third oldest of thirteen children. They went to church together, prayed together, and helped their neighbors and people in need. His father thought he would become a farmer like himself. But Angelo heard God calling him. He told his father, "I want to be a priest."

Angelo went to the seminary to study. He liked to learn about the history of the Church. He also liked to read about the lives of the saints. Some of his favorite saints were St. Joseph, St. John the Baptist, and St. Francis de Sales. Angelo was inspired by many great saints his whole life.

After he was ordained, Fr. Roncalli worked for the bishop of Bergamo as his secretary. The bishop taught Fr. Roncalli how to be a good and holy priest. He told him, "Help the poor and treat people with respect. And pray for peace, Angelo." He never forgot what the bishop told him.

A terrible war began. It was called World War I. Fr. Roncalli entered the Italian army as a military chaplain and worked at a hospital. He prayed with the soldiers who were hurt and tried to make them feel better. Fr. Roncalli prayed for peace every day.

After the war was over, Fr. Roncalli worked in the mission office. He traveled a lot and learned how people in other countries lived. He was assigned to Bulgaria as a bishop, and then as an archbishop. Later, Archbishop Roncalli was sent to help people in Turkey and Greece, where he visited poor villages by train or on horseback. The Archbishop helped people of different faiths get along with each other.

In 1944, World War II started. It was a sad time for many people. Archbishop Roncalli did not like the war. He helped thousands of men, women, and children move to other countries so they could live in peace.

The war caused problems and confusion. Archbishop Roncalli went to Paris, France after the war, to help people rebuild their lives. He helped the bishops and priests, too. His job was to help people work out their differences and bring people back to the Faith.

He was made a cardinal in 1953, and was sent to Venice, Italy. Cardinal Roncalli liked the people and the city of Venice very much. "I am seventy-two years old, and I hope this is my last assignment. I will be a good priest to my people," he said. But God had a different plan for Cardinal Roncalli!

When Pope Pius XII died in 1958, all the cardinals were called to Rome to select the next pope. Cardinal Roncalli went to Rome, too. After several votes, Cardinal Roncalli was elected pope! At first, he was a little scared. "If the other cardinals voted for me, then I accept their decision. God will be with me," he said.

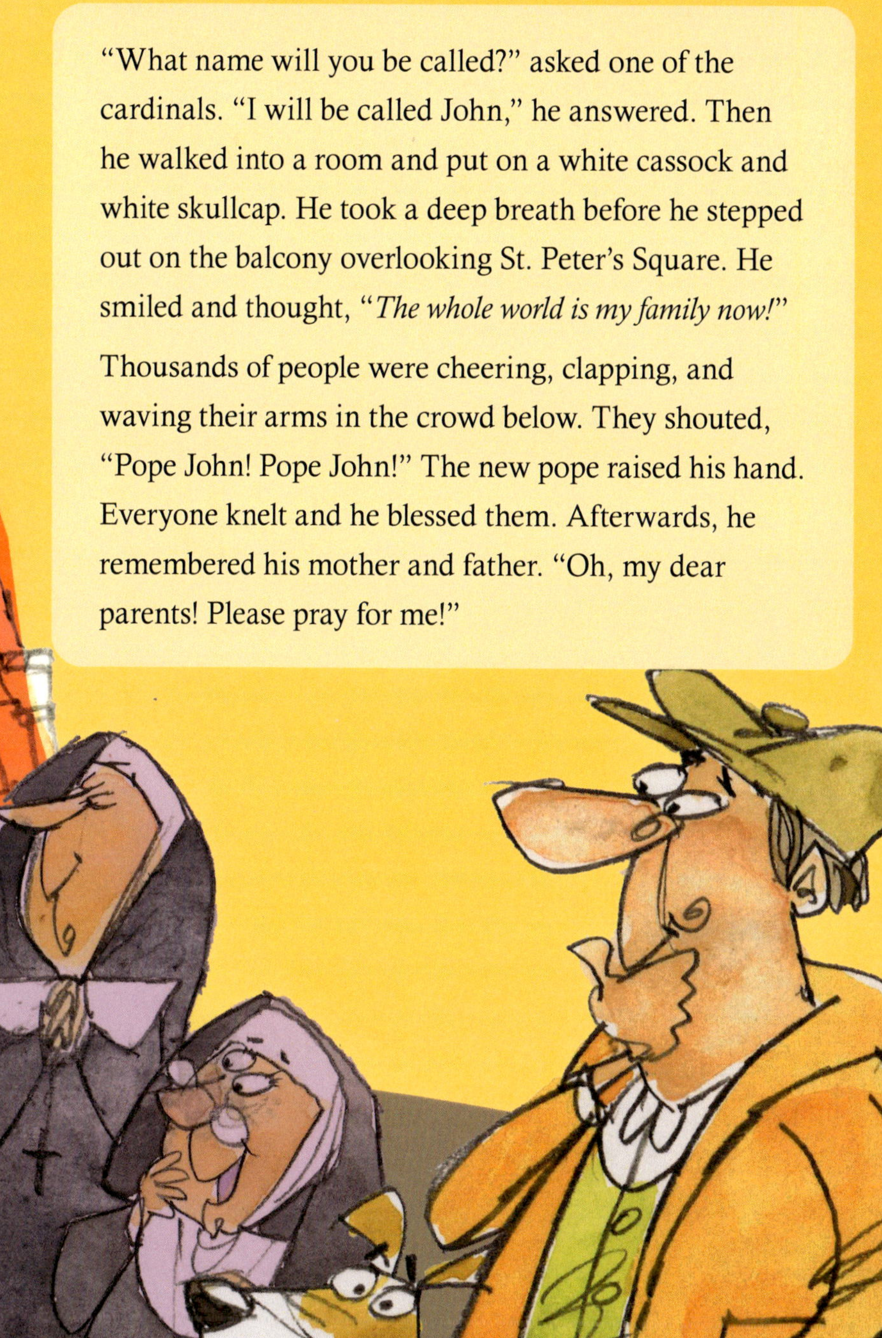

"What name will you be called?" asked one of the cardinals. "I will be called John," he answered. Then he walked into a room and put on a white cassock and white skullcap. He took a deep breath before he stepped out on the balcony overlooking St. Peter's Square. He smiled and thought, "*The whole world is my family now!*"

Thousands of people were cheering, clapping, and waving their arms in the crowd below. They shouted, "Pope John! Pope John!" The new pope raised his hand. Everyone knelt and he blessed them. Afterwards, he remembered his mother and father. "Oh, my dear parents! Please pray for me!"

Pope John XXIII liked to walk around the city and meet people. At Christmastime, he visited a children's hospital. They were so happy to see him! "God bless you, boys and girls," he said.

The next day he went to a prison. He told the men, "You cannot come to see me, so I came to see you!" He made everyone smile!

One morning after Mass, he told some priests he wanted to have a big meeting, or council, of all the cardinals in the Church. "I want to open the Church to the world and bring God's love to our brothers and sisters," he said. Some priests liked his idea. Other priests thought it was too soon for the new pope to make changes.

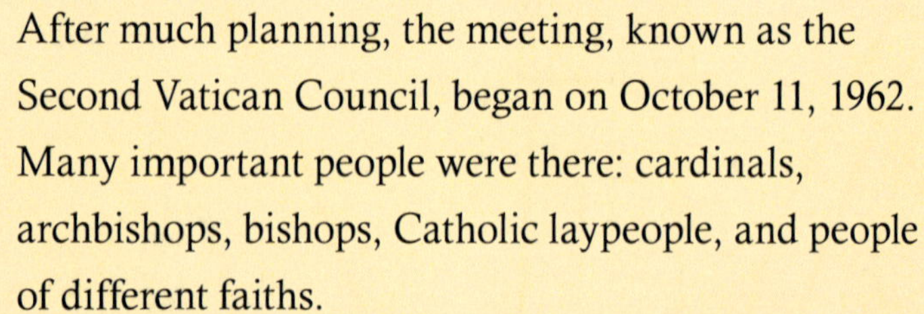

After much planning, the meeting, known as the Second Vatican Council, began on October 11, 1962. Many important people were there: cardinals, archbishops, bishops, Catholic laypeople, and people of different faiths.

The Holy Spirit guided their thoughts and discussions. They talked about how the much world had changed. It was time for the Catholic Church to change a little, too! The Church had holy work to do in the modern world.

Pope John XXIII was happy that the Second Vatican Council had started. But he was also sad because he knew he was very sick and would not live to see the good work of the council. He died on June 3, 1963. The next pope, Pope Paul VI, carried on his dream and the council ended in 1965.

People all over the world were shocked to hear the news of Pope John XXIII's death. They saw in him kindness, humor, and the goodness of God. "Good Pope John," as he was often called, gave the world a joyful message of hope and God's love.

Pope John XXIII was canonized along with Pope John Paul II on April 27, 2014, by Pope Francis. This was the first time two popes were canonized at the same time. We celebrate his feast day, not on the date that he died like most saints, but on October 11, the day the Second Vatican Council started.

Bring people together in friendship and peace,
And pray that all fighting and war will soon cease.

♥ ♥ ♥

Dear Pope Saint John,
You were God's humble and faithful servant,
and you treated people with love and respect.
Help me to serve others
with a peaceful and joyful spirit.
Amen.

GLOSSARY (NEW WORDS)

Archbishop: The bishop of an archdiocese. An archdiocese is made up of many parishes

Bishop: A priest who is the leader of many churches in a certain area

Cardinal: A member of a special group of bishops who help the pope and elect a new pope

Canonized: To officially declare that a person is a saint

Laypeople: Baptized members of the Church who give witness to Jesus Christ

Military Chaplain: One who gives spiritual and emotional care to soldiers

Ordained: To receive the sacraments of holy orders and become a deacon, priest, or bishop

Pope: The leader of the Catholic Church throughout the world

Second Vatican Council: An important meeting of bishops held from 1962 to 1965

Seminary: A school where men are trained to become priests

World War I: Also called the First World War, it was fought in Europe and the Middle East from 1914 to 1918

World War II: Also called the Second World War, much of the fighting took place in Europe and in Southeast Asia from 1939 to 1945

In 1963, Pope John XXIII wrote an *encyclical* (or important letter) titled *Peace on Earth*. His letter called for peace in a world of dangerous weapons and war.